Belongs To
_____

Starting/Ending
_____

TAKE THE PLEDGE

I **accept** that I am a *creator*.

Everything I could possibly need is AT THIS VERY MOMENT
in and about my consciousness.

I am a command center
of COURAGE, AUTHENTICITY, DECISIVENESS, and POISE
with the mental bandwidth necessary to fully activate and experience my dreams.

I create exactly what I need
to be WHOEVER I *want*.

Signature _____

Date _____

Help us and our founder, Dr. V Brooks Dunbar, achieve our goal of 1 MILLION who have taken THE CONFIDENCE COMMANDER PLEDGE to act on their dreams with courage, authenticity, decisiveness, and poise.

www.thecenterforconfidence.com
www.drvbrooksdunbar.com

My Perfect World Plan

Goal	Complete
Action 1	
Action 2	
Action 3	

Goal	Complete
Action 1	
Action 2	
Action 3	

Goal	Complete
Action 1	
Action 2	
Action 3	

Lessons learned: _____

My Perfect World Plan

_____

_____

Goal	Complete
Action 1	
Action 2	
Action 3	

Goal	Complete
Action 1	
Action 2	
Action 3	

Goal	Complete
Action 1	
Action 2	
Action 3	

Lessons learned: _____

_____

My Perfect World Plan

Goal	Complete
Action 1	
Action 2	
Action 3	

Goal	Complete
Action 1	
Action 2	
Action 3	

Goal	Complete
Action 1	
Action 2	
Action 3	

Lessons learned:

My Perfect World Plan

Goal	Complete
Action 1	
Action 2	
Action 3	

Goal	Complete
Action 1	
Action 2	
Action 3	

Goal	Complete
Action 1	
Action 2	
Action 3	

Lessons learned: _____

My Perfect World Plan

_____

_____

_____

Goal	Complete
Action 1	
Action 2	
Action 3	

Goal	Complete
Action 1	
Action 2	
Action 3	

Goal	Complete
Action 1	
Action 2	
Action 3	

Lessons learned: _____

_____

My Vision Map

My Vision Map

My Vision Map

My Vision Map

> Confidence comes
> by living life daily
> with courage, authenticity, decisiveness, and poise.
> Exercise confidence in your self, career, relationships and personal spaces
> – and success in all of these will follow.
> - Dr. V Brooks Dunbar

GET YOUR COPY:
Diva Decisions: How To Get From Smart To Intelligent
By Claiming Your Power Of Choice *(On Sale Now At Any Online Bookstore)*

Confidence is a Lifestyle. Live it!

More From Dr. V

FREE TOOLS, RESOURCES, AND DOWNLOADS AVAILABLE NOW:

- Take The Confident Lifestyle Pledge
- Take The Relational Confidence Survey
- Join The Facebook Group • Follow Dr. V's Blog & Online Channels
- "Discover Your Confidence Zones" Relational Confidence Workbook
- Quotes By Women In Power, On Women In Power

Download additional resources and products at
TheTrueDrV.club
and click on the "Bookstore & Gifts" tab.

www.thecenterforconfidence.com
www.drvbrooksdunbar.com

Confidence is a lifestyle, Live it.

Confidence is an action word. This 162-page, lined journal is designed to help women and girls bring confidence into their lives by *living life daily* with *courage, authenticity, decisiveness, and poise.*

"When you exercise confidence in your self, career, relationships and personal spaces, success in all of these will follow." –

Dr. V Brooks Dunbar

This journal includes a **"Belongs To"** page for the owner's name and an area to write in a journal start and end date. Next, start the journal by signing the **"Confidence Commander Pledge"** to live your life daily with *courage, authenticity, decisiveness, and poise.*

Then, begin to tell the story of your journey towards building confidence using the principles of courage, authenticity, decisiveness, and poise. Note challenges, actions taken to move you closer to your dreams as well as actions to overcome challenges, create goals and write out the outcomes of those goals and lessons learned, use blank pages located in the back of the journal to draw your vision maps. Sign up for updates at **www.thetruedrv.club** on Facebook to receive confidence challenges, tools, tips, and community support. Don't forget to celebrate your progress and tell everyone in your confidence circles.

To learn more about The Confidence Commander Pledge visit **www.thetruedrv.club** and become her next **#ConfidenceCrush**

www.ingramcontent.com/pod-product-compliance
Lightning Source LLC
Chambersburg PA
CBHW051547010526
44118CB00022B/2613